BOB CHILCOTT
A Little Jazz Piano

for solo piano

MUSIC DEPARTMENT

OXFORD
UNIVERSITY PRESS

for Becky and Ollie

A Little Jazz Piano

1. Bobbing along

BOB CHILCOTT

OXFORD UNIVERSITY PRESS, MUSIC DEPARTMENT, GREAT CLARENDON STREET, OXFORD OX2 6DP

3

2. Becky's Song

BOB CHILCOTT

Tender and lyrical (not swing tempo) ♩ = *c*.66

p dolce

with Ped.

3. *Walking with Ollie*

BOB CHILCOTT